Diary of a Circus Performer

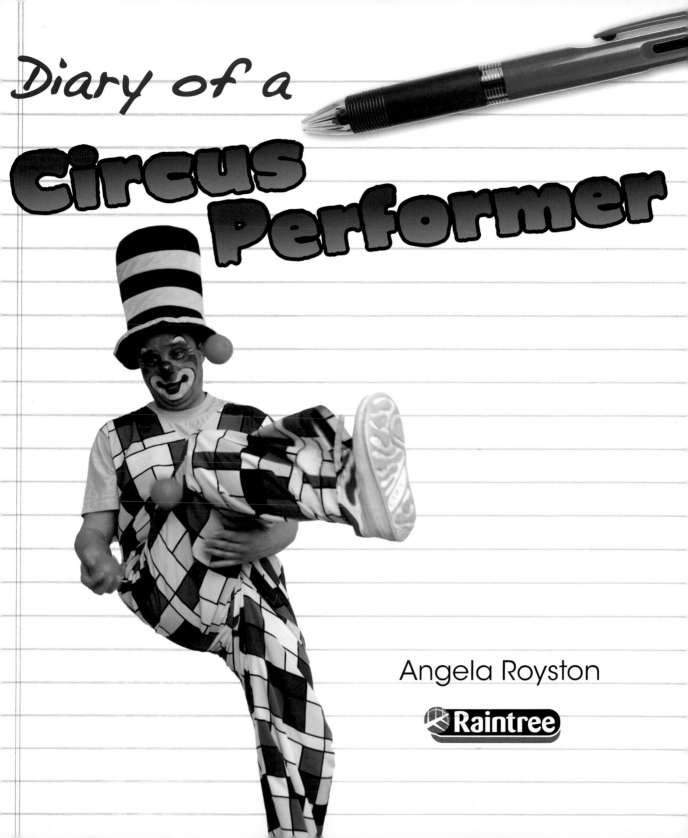

Angela Royston

Raintree

Raintree is an imprint of Capstone Global Library Limited, a company incorporated in England and Wales having its registered office at 7 Pilgrim Street, London, EC4V 6LB – Registered company number: 6695582

To contact Raintree:
Phone: 0845 6044371
Fax: + 44 (0) 1865 312263
Email: myorders@raintreepublishers.co.uk
Outside the UK please telephone +44 1865 312262

Edited by Daniel Nunn, Rebecca Rissman, and Catherine Veitch
Designed by Cynthia Della-Rovere
Picture research by Ruth Blair
Production by Victoria Fitzgerald
Originated by Capstone Global Library Ltd
Printed and bound in China by South China Printing Company Ltd

ISBN 978 1 406 26064 9
17 16 15 14 13
10 9 8 7 6 5 4 3 2 1

British Library Cataloguing in Publication Data
Royston, Angela.
Diary of a circus performer.
791.3-dc23
A full catalogue record for this book is available from the British Library.

Acknowledgements
We would like to thank the following for permission to reproduce photographs: Corbis pp. 7 (© KOEN VAN WEEL/epa), 11 (© Daniele Leone/Demotix), 12 (© Jessica Rinaldi/Reuters), 13 (© Neal Preston), 19 (© Bojan Brecelj), 21 (© John Van Hasselt); Getty Images pp. 6 (Adrian Peacock), 8 (Chip Simons), 14 (Matt Cardy), 15 (Holger Leue), 22 (LEROY Francis), 24 (Jan Sochor/Latincontent), 26 (Johannes Simon), 27 (Matt Cardy); iStockphoto p. 20 (© tomazl); Shutterstock pp. title page (© Mira Arnaudova), contents page (© Pack-Shot), 4 (© CreativeNature.nl), 5 (© Natursports), 9 (© MANDY GODBEHEAR), 16 (© Studio DMM Photography, Designs & Art), 23 (© AVAVA), 28 book (© Raulin), 28 pen (© Torsten Lorenz); Superstock pp. 10 (Ton Koene / age fotostock), 17 (Marka), 18 (age footstock), 25 (imagebroker.net).

Background and design features reproduced with permission of Shutterstock. Cover photograph of Octavio Alegria the juggler performing during the dress rehearsal of Cirque Du Soleil's Varekai show at the Royal Albert Hall in London on 5 January 2008 reproduced with permission of Getty Images (© Adrian Dennis/AFP).

We would like to thank Paul Murphy for his invaluable help in the preparation of this book.

Some words are shown in bold, **like this**. You can find out what they mean by looking in the Glossary.

Contents

Ladies and gentlemen...

I am a circus performer in a small **travelling circus**. I am a **juggler** and an **acrobat**, and this diary tells the story of one week of my life.

Many circuses have a **Big Top** like this one.

I love the circus and so do the audiences.
I can hear them gasp when I perform, but I
can't see them. I have to keep my eyes on
my juggling!

Look at that!

Saturday 20 August

Saturday is the biggest day of the week for the circus – the day when most people come to see us. This afternoon there were lots of children in the audience.

The ringmaster is in charge. He tells the audience who will perform next.

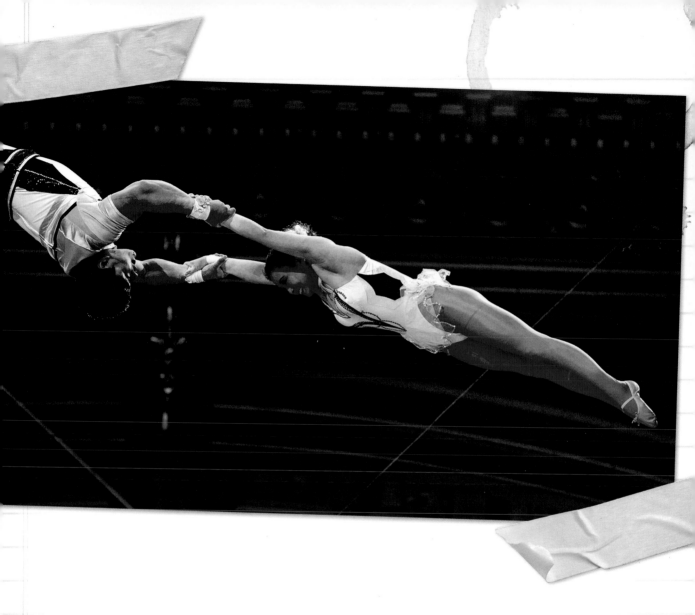

The **trapeze artists** were breathtaking. They were really high above the ground. The drums rolled and they flew through the air. The children cheered and clapped!

Hard work

Sunday 21 August

First thing this morning we all helped to clean up the litter and tidy the site. Then I practised my juggling, as I do every day.

I wanted to be an **acrobat** when I was a child because I was good at gymnastics. I joined a circus skills class and found I was even better at juggling.

Teaching the skills

Monday 22 August

Today I worked with some children who want to learn how to juggle. They started with two balls, and then I got them to try juggling with clubs.

I told them how I got started as a **juggler**. I earned money from entertaining at children's parties. I also entered juggling competitions at festivals.

Filling in

Everyone has to do lots of jobs in a circus. I was checking tickets this afternoon. It's great seeing all the children coming to see the show. They always look very excited!

tightrope walker

This evening I dressed in a **spangled** costume and helped the tightrope walkers. I threw **props** up to them as they balanced on the rope. I had to aim carefully!

New look

Tuesday 23 August

The ringmaster said my act needed a new look. So, I'm going to change it. Today I designed myself a new costume.

I've also been practising some new **stunts** for my act. I'm going to mix some acrobatic tricks with the juggling.

After the show

Tomorrow we move to a new town, so we started to clear up as soon as the show was over. We sold lots of tickets this week, and the owner was very happy!

The clowns were very popular – they always are. They might look like they are just fooling around, but they have to practise lots!

Packing up

Wednesday 24 August

Everyone worked together to take down the **Big Top** and pack up all the **wagons**. We're used to doing this, so we worked as fast as we could.

Robanito

Can you guess who this wagon belongs to?

I helped to fold up the Big Top. It was hard work! Then it was loaded onto a truck. The circus is always on the move. I often miss being at home with my family.

On the move

We set off to the next town. I drove my **camper van** and followed the **wagon** in front. The camper van is small but it's my home!

Putting up the **Big Top** is hard work.

When we arrived, it all began again. We unloaded and started to set up the site. Then we had some food. Now it's late and I'm so tired!

Problems!

Thursday 25 August

Setting up the circus is even harder than packing it up! And today we had an extra problem. The tightrope walker had to go home because her mum was very ill.

The owner told me I had to take over – but not on the **high wire**, thank goodness! He knows I like acrobatics. I stopped what I was doing and started practising!

How was I?

I was so nervous before my performance. The music began and I cartwheeled into the ring. I did some **stunts** on the rope ladder and then some balances on metal poles.

Then I started juggling hoops. The audience loved it. Afterwards the owner said I was amazing and very talented. He was right – I saved the show!

What next?

Friday 26 August

If I am so talented, maybe I should apply to work in a bigger circus! **Cirque du Soleil** is one of the best. If I worked for them, I could get to travel abroad.

This **acrobat** performs in the Cirque du Soleil.

Gerry Cottle's was an old circus that is still famous today.

No, I think I'll stay here for a few more years. I'll practise and improve my skills. People who work together in a circus are like a family. I don't want to leave my circus family yet.

Writing a diary

You can write a diary too! Your diary can describe your life – what you saw, what you felt, and the events that happened.

You could write a diary with your friends about an event that you all enjoyed. Each write something about the event. Then read out your entries to each other.

Work hard and you might become a star writer one day!

Here are some tips for writing a diary:

- Start each entry with the day and the date. You don't have to include an entry for every day.

- The entries should be in **chronological** order, which means that they follow the order in which events happened.

- Use the past tense when you are writing about something that has already happened.

- Remember that a diary is the writer's story, so use "I" and "my".

Glossary

acrobat person who performs difficult stunts with their body, such as balancing on one hand

Big Top very large tent in which a circus performs

camper van large van that includes bunk beds, kitchen, and living area

chronological in order of time

Cirque du Soleil famous Canadian circus with many acrobats and other performers. The name means Circus of the Sun.

high wire wire that tightrope walkers use. It is fixed high above the ground.

juggler someone who throws up and catches several objects after each other

props objects needed for a particular performance

spangled covered with small circles of shining metal

stunt act that catches people's attention

trapeze artist circus acrobat who performs on a swing at the top of the Big Top

travelling circus circus that travels from place to place to perform

wagon large trailer or truck. In a circus, seats and other equipment are stored in wagons, and other wagons are used as an office or kitchen, and so on.

Find out more

Books

Circus Performer (Stage School), Lisa Regan (Windmill Books, 2012)

Circus Skills (Starstruck), Cathy West (Ransom, 2011)

Circus Skills (Super Skills), Stephanie Turnbull (Hachette Children's Books, 2012)

Websites

www.circusarts.org.uk/i-want-to/learn-circus-skills/index.php
This website tells you where there are circus classes in the United Kingdom.

www.cirquedusoleil.com/en/welcome.aspx
Cirque du Soleil has circuses in every country and employs 4,000 people in many different circuses. The official website shows video clips and tells you about the history of the circus.

ethemes.missouri.edu/themes/1286
This website has links to other websites that tell you about what it's like to be a circus performer, and gives you information about particular circuses.

Index